A STREAM OF THOUGHTS

GUNEET KAUR KAHLON

Made with ♥ on the Notion Press Platform
www.notionpress.com

*This book is dedicated to every person out there who has different thoughts running in his/her mind 24*7 just like me.*

Contents

Foreword

I'm a 13-year-old poet. I started my writing journey the previous year when I was 12 during the lockdown. I did not know about this talent of mine until I was added to a school group of 'Orators and Writers' in which we were given topics on which we had to write articles or compositions. I wasn't serious about it back then. But whenever I used to sit down to write something I enjoyed that time. After a few months, I was offered to get published in a book by my school teacher. I was elated. The topic was related to school memories. That was the time when I tried my hands at poetry. I didn't know how to compose poems but the only thing I had in my mind was that joining the rhyming words will make up a poem. And this thing did work and I wrote my first ever poem 'Teacher: A Blessing' which I've added to this book as well. I composed this poem within 30 minutes. I also got the poem published which was a massive thing for me. I felt proud of myself. Especially the happy faces of my family were everything to me. After that, I also got another poem published which was 'Covid Covid Go Away' which also has been added to this book. And now after getting published two times this is my third time but this time I'm getting a whole book published which is a huge thing for me. I'm blissful.

Preface

In this book, I've added all the poems that I've composed from the previous year to now. This book contains poems composed by me on different topics according to my experiences, observations, and thoughts. My observation during covid has been summed up in the form of a poem. What do family, friends, and teachers mean to me, I've composed a poem on that as well. My thoughts about life, food, nature, and everything have been added to this book in the form of a poem. Everyone has different opinions and I've put my perception related to different things in this book.

Preface

In this book, I've added all the poems that I've composed from the previous year to now. This book contains poems composed [illegible] different [illegible] ding my experiences [illegible] My observations during covid has have [illegible] poem. What [illegible] me, and [illegible] a poem [illegible] well. My [illegible] this book [illegible] [illegible] my perception [illegible] [illegible] book.

Acknowledgements

A big thanks to my teacher who gave me wings to fly high in writing. Without her recognition, I wouldn't have even known about this hidden talent of mine. Also, I would like to thank my parents for supporting and believing in me. Without the support and encouragement of my parents, nothing is possible and I wouldn't have been able to do anything without them. I would thank my sister as well. She plays a really important role in everything I do.

Prologue

Have a good time reading the book,

You can read out about my situation during covid because obviously of it, you can't have a look.

An introduction to my family,

My love for food which I eat happily.

The maddest people alive,

Also what happens when you don't strive?

The life which goes never as planned,

Another beautiful friend.

The arrival of another year,

Your second mother is a Teacher.

A memorable vacation,

My hobbies and since birth 13 years of completion.

1. Covid Covid Go Away

I can't stay in anymore,
Can't stay away from school anyhow.
Covid Covid stay away,
Covid Covid go away.
Due to you, many are losing lives,
Earlier they were killed with knives.
Covid Covid stay away,
Covid Covid go away.
Many have lost their jobs,
Everyone no matter male or female is picking mops.
Covid Covid stay away,
Covid Covid go away.
All are missing going out,
All are clicking pics inside the house by making a pout.
Covid Covid stay away,
Covid Covid go away.
This mask is a new tradition,
Earlier we used to apply sunscreen to protect ourselves from ultra-virus radiation.
Covid Covid stay away,
Covid Covid go away.
Everyone is fed up with sitting at home,
No one would ask for a holiday anymore.

Covid Covid stay away,
Covid Covid go away.
Everywhere I'm hearing about corona these days,
Due to this everyone is dealing with online pays.
Covid Covid stay away,
Covid Covid go away.
Everyone is full of negativity,
We all are doing only indoor activity.
Covid Covid stay away,
Covid Covid go away.
Online classes are not great now,
I want to go back to school right now.
Covid Covid stay away,
Covid Covid go away.
I'm privileged that I'm having all the resources with me,
But let's help those who are needy by keeping bullies aside.
Covid Covid stay away,
Covid Covid go away.
However, we're getting punished due to our negligence,
Now everyone is protecting themselves by creating a fence.
Covid Covid stay away,
Covid Covid go away.
I don't know how this hard time will go,
But my prayers will continue.
Covid Covid stay away,
Covid Covid go away.

2. Family: Everything

Let me introduce you to my family,
My beautiful mother who always lives happily,
One who bounds the family and is always lively,
She has a lot of pain in her heart but still acts funny.
My father: A superhero of mine,
In my eyes the one who'll always shine,
He always does things before time,
He can suffer through anything but he'll never let his family suffer anytime.
A helping hand to me,
The one who treats me as a baby,
Together we're crazy,
My sister: as important as a mother and father in a family.
All three are the greatest support pillars of my life,
If I give up, they motivate me and I can do it they make me believe,
They always consider me a gift in their life,
But they don't know they only are my life.
Other than us we consider God our biggest member of the family,
Due to whom we're always happy,
We are always thankful for his countless blessings and love,
Thank you for everything our beloved one!

3. Food: The reason I'm chubby

My love for food is exceptional,
I want everything to be edible.
*24*7 I'm thinking about food,*
This is the only thing that improves my mood.
I want to eat and eat and again eat,
But without getting plumpy and that's it.
From sour to sweet and then from savory to spicy,
I can eat it all that too without being dicey.
I try to avoid junk food,
But the food itself can't stay without me maybe because I'm too good.
If there's any special occasion,
According to me, the food menu should be decided before anything else because after that only I'll get relaxation.
Eating is the key to my happiness,
But due to eating a lot what doesn't fit me is my favorite dress.
Now I will eat healthy to get fit,
But once in a while maybe I can have junk food because I love it.

4. Friends Are Forever

Not all relations are blood-related,
Some are much more than that and friendship is one such created.
Talking and sharing your problems with them gives another level of relaxation,
To describe this bond there's no abbreviation.
In the middle of class, we're always giggling,
Over the tiniest things, we're quarreling.
No matter how much we fight,
In the end, we're together and solve our fight by giving a hug that is tight.
I can't even imagine a day without my friends,
Whenever in trouble they're the ones always there to defend.
We're creating memories together for a lifetime,
We're available to each other anywhere and anytime.
Our never-ending talks,
With long walks.
They're the ones who make you laugh even if you're sad,
And you'll forget that when you met them you were in a mood which was bad.

5. When You Don't Strive

Ugh! It changed my life,
This is the expression when you don't strive.
Getting failed and experiencing something that I never had,
Yes, I'm afraid of that.
But it's important to experience failure and make mistakes,
But also, that's the path that I never want to take.
I'm afraid to know what'll happen if I fail only when I don't try,
Will I cry?
I know no one can get rid of these experiences,
This is a path of difficulties.
It only appears when you don't strive,
Now you need to survive.
When you land on this stage,
Take it as an advantage.
Why? Because it will teach you a lot,
If ever you face something like this again then you can remember in front of your difficulties how you fought.
Try hard and come back from this phase of life,
And then forever continue to strive,
Keep the practicing spirit alive in you all the time,
If you ever experience this again don't get sad because this experience is for a lifetime,
It's only there when you don't strive.

6. Life is Never as Planned

Life is just so unpredictable,
But for sure it can never be undesirable.
There are going to be highs and lows,
Some moments are fast and some are slow.
You'll always accept success but also need to learn to accept failure,
A failure is a success in progress which will make you rise and shine.
Why don't we think about the happy moments when we're sad?
Life teaches you to be both depressed and glad.
If a heartbeat is up and down that means the person is alive,
In the same way, there have to be highs and lows and that's the fun of life.
Always cherish the moments, don't always run behind something more,
Because afterward, you'll regret running behind something more.
Find happiness in small things,
Because there are also people who live happily having nothing.
Life is the biggest teacher,
If you'll be a good student then it will be your turn to be a leader.

7. Nature: The Best Place

Over time I've realized,
Nature is the best place and it needs to be emphasized.
The greenery is mesmerizing,
Every time the view is awestruck even when the sun is rising.
It is the coziest place,
The best of all is its Grace.
Day by day we're destroying Nature,
But showing us its wonders, which shows it's such a kind creature.
I'm obsessed with it, just want to stare at it the whole day,
To appreciate it I've thousands of words to say.
This is the best gift anyone can get,
There's nothing better than this, I bet.
I'm just so thankful for its existence,
When you'll observe it, for my words used for it, you'll have all the evidence.
Nurture Nature,
To save the future.

8. New Year, New Begginings

2023 is about to arrive,
Give me a high five.
Let's prepare a wish list again for the upcoming year,
Also, with some wishes that were not completed this year.
We'll build up some new habits,
Also, Pack all the bad deeds in packets.
Learn to be truthful,
As well as grateful.
Start the year with a big smile,
All the memories from the previous year just compile.
Help the needy to make their new year special,
Because it's not illegal.
Let's forget past mistakes,
Teaching you something was its sake.
Groove that night with new cheer,
Wish you a happy new year!
Let's just hope for fulfillment, Contentment, peace, and more,
A brighter, better new year than we've ever had before.

9. Teacher: A Blessing

Teachers are a true blessing,
Like a mother she's caring.
They're a second mother to all of us,
They clear the doubts even traveling in a bus.
Teaching is the priority for them,
They're truly a gem.
Never makes the class boring,
Every time she's adoring.
She is quite sometimes strict,
To shout in class, she often restricts.
She is the epitome of goodness and kindness,
Teaches us that doesn't matter how much knowledge you acquire
it's always the less.
She's always smiling,
To teach she's always willing.
A child can never thank a teacher,
Can pray that may God give her a life that is larger.

10. Trip to Manali

Was so excited just a night before,
Had just heard about its beauty before but now wanted to explore.
Earlier won't wake up before 8 at least,
But now the sleep of 7-8 hours didn't want to complete.
Started traveling with enthusiasm,
A little later mountain was welcomed.
A long journey just went by sleeping and sightseeing,
Also, with a lot of eating.
The beauty of the hills just amazed me,
Can't even describe its beauty with words such as pretty.
The first stop was to seek blessings from God,
Visited a Gurudwara and Temple to praise the lord.
The night view was amazing,
In the local market of Manikaran, we were wandering.
The Next day enrooted to Manali with a lot more excitement,
Experienced such a view in 'Kullu' which was completely different.
The beauty of the 'Beas' River was Mesmerizing,
The gorgeousness of nature there I was realizing.
Just didn't want to get out of there,
To visit it was such a pleasure.
Then finally came Manali after a long journey of hours,

Which had extreme powers.
Shopped a lot from the 'Mall Road',
Ate a lot of street food which made me explode.
Another day and another visit to 'Rohtang' with the hope to play with snow,
As soon as we reached seeing the snow on my face there was a glow.
Slowly and steadily reached the top,
Seeing the breathtaking view, I did stop.
Of course, how can one forget having 'Maggi' when in the mountains,
After hours of enjoyment going back was certain.
Came back to Manali and explored the streets on the last night,
This trip was truly a delight.

11. What do I love doing

Of course, this has to be the one, and that too topmost one,
Composing poems is what I love and it's also fun.
I love writing down my observation,
In the form of a poem that can be based on any situation.
Who doesn't like grooving?
Because it's so soothing.
I don't like exercising but burning calories in this way are fun,
It's better than going out to run.
Discovered this one lately,
But I think so far I've been doing art and craft greatly.
Each day I'm getting better,
Others may not like it but for me, my efforts do matter.
Spending time with family and playing cards or games,
Gaining knowledge from books.
Also playing 'Teacher-Teacher' which is now a thing,
This is all that I love doing.

12. What does it feel to be entering teenage

I've mixed emotions going on,
I can't believe it's going to be 13 years since the day I was born.
Sometimes, I feel like conquering the world,
There are also days when I feel like doing nothing, It's all tangled.
I would cry over the silliest things like a baby,
And also laugh like anything being crazy.
There are days when I don't want to talk,
Also, there are days when I won't stop talking even when I'm tired due to a long walk.
Although, I'm feeling responsible,
I've also kinda become sensible.
I don't know how life after entering teenage would be,
But I would try to set my mind tension-free.
I'm a little nervous as well as excited about this phase,
To know about this phase there's a wait of a few days.
I wish myself nothing but luck for a new phase in my life,
Doesn't matter what I'll always strive.

Printed by Libri Plureos GmbH in Hamburg,
Germany